4M AI MODEL
Apple's Secret Power Behind the Next Tech Boom

Discover How This Revolutionary Technology Will Transform Everything from Creativity to Security

Alejandro S. Diego

Copyright © Alejandro S. Diego, 2024.

All rights reserved. No part of this publication may be reproduced, distributed, or transmitted in any form or by any means, including photocopying, recording, or other electronic or mechanical methods, without the prior written permission of the publisher, except in the case of brief quotations embodied in critical reviews and certain other noncommercial uses permitted by copyright law.

Table of Contents

Introduction 4
Chapter 1: The Genesis of the 4M AI Model 7
Chapter 2: Understanding the 4M AI Model 15
Chapter 3: Transforming Industries with 4M AI 25
Chapter 4: Enhancing Everyday Technology 36
Chapter 5: Accessibility and Inclusivity 47
1. Verbal Descriptions for Visually Impaired Users. 53
2. Adaptation to Various User Needs and Preferences 55
Chapter 6: Data Privacy and Security 59
Chapter 7: The Public Launch and Community Impact 65
Chapter 8: The Market Impact of 4M AI 71
Chapter 9: The Future of 4M AI and Beyond 78
Conclusion 87

Introduction

Imagine a world where your thoughts can shape reality, where the boundaries between imagination and creation blur, and where the future of technology lies not just in our hands but in our very words. Apple's latest innovation, the 4M AI Model, is more than just another advancement in artificial intelligence; it is a revolution poised to redefine the very fabric of our interaction with technology. This is not just an upgrade—it's a paradigm shift, a leap into a new era where possibilities expand beyond our wildest dreams.

At its core, the 4M AI Model, or the Massively Multimodal Mask Modeling system, represents a breakthrough that many believed was still decades away. This technology does not merely understand language, process images, or analyze data in isolated silos. Instead, it integrates these elements into a unified system that can think, see, and even visualize in three dimensions, much like a human mind. The implications of such a system are profound, offering a glimpse into a future where creativity, security, and even the most mundane tasks are transformed into something extraordinary.

For decades, artificial intelligence has been on a steady path of evolution, improving incrementally with each passing year. But the 4M AI Model is a game-changer, setting a new standard for what we can expect from AI in the coming years. Whether you're a creative professional seeking to push the boundaries of your work, a security expert looking to safeguard the digital realm, or simply someone intrigued by the next big thing in technology, this model promises to deliver in ways that were once the stuff of science fiction.

As we delve into the intricacies of this groundbreaking technology, we'll explore not just what the 4M AI Model is, but what it means for the future. This book will guide you through the vast landscape of possibilities that this model unlocks, from revolutionizing industries to reshaping our everyday lives. The journey you are about to embark on is one filled with innovation, discovery, and a deeper understanding of how Apple's 4M AI Model is set to change the world as we know it.

Prepare to be captivated, intrigued, and perhaps even a little awestruck as we unravel the secrets behind one of the most exciting technological advancements of our time. The pages that follow will not only inform you but will inspire you to think about the limitless potential that lies ahead. Welcome to the future of artificial intelligence, where the impossible becomes possible, and where Apple's 4M AI Model stands as the beacon lighting the way.

Chapter 1: The Genesis of the 4M AI Model

Apple's journey in artificial intelligence has been marked by a careful blend of innovation, secrecy, and a relentless pursuit of excellence. From the early days of integrating machine learning into its products, Apple has consistently aimed to make AI more intuitive, more personal, and more embedded into the fabric of everyday life. The development of Siri, Apple's voice assistant, was one of the first public glimpses into the company's commitment to AI, showcasing a future where technology could understand and respond to human commands in a more natural way. But this was just the beginning.

Over the years, Apple has gradually infused AI into nearly every aspect of its ecosystem. From the sophisticated image recognition in Photos that allows users to search for memories with a few keywords, to the predictive text and contextual suggestions that anticipate what you need before you even realize it, Apple has been quietly building an AI infrastructure that is both powerful and seamless. However, this approach, while effective, was only the foundation for something far greater.

The development of the 4M AI Model marks a significant leap forward in Apple's AI strategy. Unlike previous models, which focused on specific tasks such as image recognition or natural language processing, the 4M AI Model integrates multiple modalities—text, images, audio, and even 3D spatial data—into a single, cohesive system. This integration allows the 4M AI Model to understand and generate outputs across various formats, making it a truly multimodal AI system. But Apple didn't achieve this breakthrough on its own.

In a departure from its traditionally secretive approach, Apple embarked on a collaboration with the Swiss Federal Institute of Technology, one of the world's leading research institutions, and Hugging Face, a prominent open-source AI platform. This partnership was not only strategic but also symbolic, signaling a new era of openness and collaboration in AI research. The Swiss Federal Institute of Technology brought cutting-edge academic research to the table, while Hugging Face provided the infrastructure and community engagement needed to refine and test the model in real-world scenarios.

This collaboration allowed Apple to tap into a broader range of expertise and perspectives, accelerating the development of the 4M AI Model. By working with these partners, Apple was able to push the boundaries of what was possible, creating a model that is not just an evolution of existing technology, but a complete reimagining of what AI can do. The result is a system that is not only capable of performing tasks across different modalities but does so with a level of sophistication and accuracy that sets a new standard in the industry.

As we continue to explore the impact of the 4M AI Model, it's important to recognize that this achievement is the culmination of years of quiet innovation, strategic collaboration, and a vision of the future where technology enhances, rather than complicates, our lives. Apple's journey in AI has been a steady ascent, and with the 4M AI Model, the company has reached a new pinnacle, setting the stage for a future where the boundaries between the digital and physical worlds blur in ways we are only beginning to understand.

The path to the 4M AI Model is one of incremental innovation, visionary thinking, and a relentless pursuit of technological excellence. Apple's journey to creating this groundbreaking AI system was not a sudden leap but a carefully orchestrated series of developments that built upon each other over time. Each step along the way contributed to the creation of a model that is now set to redefine how we interact with technology.

The development process for the 4M AI Model began with a clear recognition of the limitations inherent in traditional AI systems. Early AI models were often designed to excel in specific tasks—like recognizing faces in photos or transcribing speech into text. While these models were impressive in their own right, they operated in isolation, each handling only one type of data or performing one kind of task. Apple recognized that to truly push the boundaries of artificial intelligence, a new approach was needed—one that could seamlessly integrate multiple forms of data into a unified system.

This realization led to the concept of multimodal AI, where different types of data—text, images, audio, and spatial information—could be processed together. Apple's engineers and researchers began exploring how to create a system that could not only understand these diverse forms of data but also generate meaningful outputs that combined them in new and innovative ways. This was no small feat, as it required the development of sophisticated algorithms capable of handling the complexity and diversity of multimodal inputs.

One of the key technological advancements that made the 4M AI Model possible was Apple's progress in machine learning and neural networks. Over the years, Apple invested heavily in refining its machine learning models, ensuring they could handle increasingly complex tasks with greater accuracy. The introduction of the Neural Engine in Apple's custom chips was a significant milestone, providing the necessary computational power to support advanced AI tasks directly on devices. This hardware innovation was crucial in enabling the 4M AI Model to perform in real-time, without relying on cloud processing, which in turn enhanced user privacy and security.

Another critical aspect of the 4M AI Model's development was the integration of natural language processing (NLP) with computer vision and spatial reasoning. Apple's researchers worked to develop algorithms that could understand and generate human language, recognize objects and scenes in images, and interpret three-dimensional spaces. This multidisciplinary approach allowed the 4M AI Model to function more like a human brain, processing and synthesizing information from multiple sources to create a coherent understanding of the world.

Throughout this process, Apple remained committed to ensuring that the 4M AI Model was not only powerful but also accessible. The model was designed to be intuitive and user-friendly, enabling even those without technical expertise to harness its capabilities. This focus on accessibility was reflected in the design of the model's user interface and the simplicity with which users could interact with it, whether they were generating images from text descriptions or manipulating 3D scenes through natural language commands.

As the 4M AI Model took shape, Apple continued to refine and test the system, ensuring that it met the company's high standards for performance and reliability. The collaboration with external partners, such as the Swiss Federal Institute of Technology and Hugging Face, played a crucial role in this phase, providing valuable insights and feedback that helped Apple fine-tune the model. The result of this meticulous development process was a system that not only pushed the boundaries of what AI could achieve but also set a new standard for how AI could be integrated into everyday life.

The evolution to the 4M AI Model is a testament to Apple's ability to blend cutting-edge technology with a deep understanding of user needs. By bringing together advancements in machine learning, natural language processing, computer vision, and spatial reasoning, Apple has created a model that is both powerful and practical. The 4M AI Model is not just an evolution in AI; it represents a revolution in how we will interact with technology in the years to come.

Chapter 2: Understanding the 4M AI Model

The 4M AI Model, or "Massively Multimodal Mask Modeling," is a revolutionary system designed to process and integrate multiple types of data into a single, cohesive framework. Unlike traditional AI models that typically focus on a single type of input, such as text or images, the 4M AI Model can handle a variety of data formats simultaneously. This capability allows the model to understand, interpret, and generate outputs that blend these diverse forms of information in ways that were previously unimaginable.

At its core, the 4M system is built on the concept of multimodality, which refers to the ability to process different types of data—text, images, 3D data, and spatial information—together. The "Mask Modeling" aspect of the system refers to the sophisticated algorithms that allow the AI to selectively focus on specific parts of the input data, masking out irrelevant details and highlighting the most important features. This technique enables the model to generate highly accurate and contextually relevant outputs, whether it's creating an image from a text description or manipulating a 3D scene based on verbal commands.

One of the most striking features of the 4M AI Model is its ability to create images from text descriptions. For example, if a user provides a detailed description of a sunset over mountains with a lake in the foreground, the 4M system can generate an image that accurately reflects this scene. This capability is made possible by the model's integration of text and image data, allowing it to translate linguistic information into visual representations. This feature is incredibly useful for professionals in creative industries, such as graphic design and marketing, where rapid visual content generation is often required.

Beyond text and images, the 4M AI Model also excels in handling 3D data and spatial information. This means the system can not only recognize objects within a three-dimensional space but also manipulate that space based on user input. For instance, an architect could describe a building design, and the model would generate a 3D model of the building, allowing for real-time adjustments and visualizations. This capability is particularly valuable in fields like architecture, game development, and virtual reality, where the ability to quickly and accurately manipulate 3D environments is essential.

The integration of spatial information adds another layer of complexity to the 4M AI Model's capabilities. Spatial information refers to the data related to the position, size, and orientation of objects within a given space. By incorporating this data, the 4M system can understand how different elements in a scene relate to each other, enabling it to generate more accurate and contextually appropriate outputs. For example, in an augmented reality application, the model could place a virtual object in a real-world environment with the correct scale and perspective, making the virtual object appear as if it naturally belongs in the scene.

What sets the 4M AI Model apart is its unified architecture, which seamlessly integrates these different types of data into a single system. This integration allows the model to perform tasks that would typically require multiple specialized tools, streamlining workflows and enhancing productivity. Users can interact with the 4M AI Model using natural language, making it accessible to a broader audience, including those without technical expertise. This democratization of advanced AI technology is one of the key aspects of the 4M system, as it opens up new possibilities for innovation and creativity across various industries.

The 4M AI Model is more than just a technological advancement; it represents a new way of thinking about how AI can be used to solve complex problems. By integrating text, images, 3D data, and spatial information into a single, powerful system, Apple has created a tool that has the potential to transform industries and redefine how we interact with the digital world. Whether it's enhancing creative workflows, improving security systems, or enabling more immersive virtual experiences, the 4M AI Model is poised to make a significant impact on the future of technology.

One of the most remarkable features of the 4M AI Model is its ability to generate images from text descriptions, a capability that pushes the boundaries of what artificial intelligence can achieve. This feature enables users to create detailed and accurate visual representations simply by describing them in words. For instance, if you were to describe a serene scene of a sunset over a mountain range with a lake reflecting the golden hues of the sky, the 4M AI Model could instantly generate an image that captures this vision. This ability to translate language into images is not just a novelty; it is a powerful tool for professionals who rely on visual content. Graphic designers, marketers, and content creators, who often require rapid production of visual assets, can benefit immensely from this feature, bypassing the need for extensive design expertise or time-consuming manual creation processes.

The underlying technology that enables this image generation from text is the model's integration of natural language processing with advanced computer vision algorithms. By understanding the nuances of language and how it relates to visual elements, the 4M AI Model can create images that are not only accurate but also artistically compelling. This capability opens up new possibilities for creative expression, allowing users to bring their ideas to life with unprecedented ease and precision.

In addition to its image generation prowess, the 4M AI Model excels in complex object detection, a feature that is particularly useful in applications requiring precise and rapid identification of objects within images or videos. Object detection is the process by which the AI can identify and categorize various elements within a visual scene, recognizing specific objects, understanding their context, and determining their relevance. This capability is crucial in industries such as security and surveillance, where the ability to detect unauthorized access or suspicious behavior in real-time can be a game-changer.

For example, in a security system, the 4M AI Model can analyze live footage to detect specific activities, such as a person entering a restricted area or an unattended bag left in a public space. The model's accuracy in object detection ensures that it can distinguish between benign and potentially harmful situations, reducing false alarms and improving overall security. In healthcare, this same technology can be applied to medical imaging, where the model can identify anomalies or conditions with a high degree of precision, aiding in early diagnosis and treatment planning. The speed and accuracy of the 4M AI Model in object detection make it an invaluable tool across various industries, where the stakes are often high, and the need for reliable results is critical.

Another standout feature of the 4M AI Model is its ability to manipulate 3D scenes through natural language input. This means that users can describe changes they want to see in a three-dimensional environment, and the AI will implement those changes in real-time. This capability is particularly transformative for fields like architecture, game development, and virtual reality, where the ability to quickly and accurately modify 3D environments is essential.

Imagine an architect working on a new building design. Instead of manually adjusting the 3D model through traditional software, they could simply describe the changes they want—perhaps moving a wall, adjusting the height of a ceiling, or adding new elements to the design—and the 4M AI Model would make these adjustments instantly. This not only speeds up the design process but also allows for more iterative and creative experimentation, as users can see the results of their ideas in real-time and make adjustments on the fly.

For game developers, this feature can revolutionize the way game environments are created and modified. By using natural language to manipulate 3D scenes, developers can quickly build and tweak game worlds, creating more immersive and interactive experiences for players. The ability to seamlessly integrate natural language with 3D manipulation makes the 4M AI Model a powerful tool for enhancing creativity and productivity in industries where visual and spatial design are paramount.

The 4M AI Model's key features—image generation from text, complex object detection, and manipulation of 3D scenes—are all underpinned by its advanced multimodal capabilities. By integrating text, images, and spatial data into a unified system, Apple has created an AI model that not only performs these tasks with remarkable accuracy but also makes them accessible to users across various fields. Whether you're a creative professional, a security expert, or a developer, the 4M AI Model provides the tools you need to take your work to the next level, transforming the way you interact with technology and opening up new possibilities for innovation.

Chapter 3: Transforming Industries with 4M AI

The 4M AI Model is poised to revolutionize the creative industries in profound ways, transforming the processes of graphic design, marketing, and content creation. Traditionally, these fields have relied heavily on human creativity and labor-intensive workflows to produce visual and textual content. However, with the introduction of the 4M AI Model, these industries are experiencing a paradigm shift, where advanced technology not only enhances creative output but also redefines the very nature of creativity itself.

In the realm of graphic design, the 4M AI Model is a game-changer. Designers have long been limited by the tools at their disposal, often requiring significant time and effort to produce high-quality visual content. The 4M AI Model changes this dynamic by allowing designers to generate images directly from text descriptions. This capability means that a designer can now simply describe the vision they have in mind—whether it's a complex scene, a specific style, or a particular color scheme—and the AI will generate an image that matches the description. This not only speeds up the design process but also allows designers to experiment with different concepts rapidly, enabling a level of creative exploration that was previously impractical.

Moreover, the 4M AI Model's ability to integrate text and image data opens up new possibilities for creating visually compelling designs that are also contextually relevant. For example, a designer working on a campaign for a new product can use the AI to generate images that not only look stunning but also convey the desired message or evoke the right emotions. This capability bridges the gap between visual aesthetics and communication, ensuring that the final design resonates with the intended audience on multiple levels.

In marketing, the 4M AI Model offers unprecedented opportunities for personalization and engagement. Marketers have always sought to create content that speaks directly to their target audience, but doing so effectively has often been a challenge due to the diversity of consumer preferences and behaviors. The 4M AI Model addresses this by enabling the creation of highly personalized content at scale. By analyzing data on consumer preferences, the AI can generate marketing materials—be it images, videos, or text—that are tailored to individual tastes and interests. This level of personalization not only increases the effectiveness of marketing campaigns but also fosters a deeper connection between brands and consumers.

The AI's ability to produce high-quality visual content quickly also means that marketers can respond to trends and opportunities in real-time. For instance, if a brand wants to capitalize on a viral social media trend, the 4M AI Model can generate relevant content almost instantly, allowing the brand to engage with its audience in a timely and impactful manner. This agility is crucial in today's fast-paced digital landscape, where the ability to stay ahead of the curve can make or break a marketing campaign.

Content creation, in general, stands to benefit immensely from the 4M AI Model's capabilities. Content creators, whether they are bloggers, video producers, or social media influencers, often face the challenge of producing fresh, engaging content on a consistent basis. The 4M AI Model eases this burden by providing a powerful tool for generating content quickly and efficiently. For example, a content creator could use the AI to generate images for a blog post, create video content with automated editing features, or even write compelling copy based on brief input. This not only saves time but also allows creators to focus more on their creative vision rather than the technical aspects of content production.

The integration of 3D data and spatial information into the 4M AI Model also opens up new avenues for immersive content creation. Virtual reality (VR) and augmented reality (AR) experiences, which are becoming increasingly popular in marketing and entertainment, can be significantly enhanced by the AI's ability to manipulate 3D scenes through natural language. Content creators can now design and modify VR or AR environments more easily, bringing their imaginative worlds to life with greater precision and realism.

The impact of the 4M AI Model on the creative industries is profound and far-reaching. By automating many of the technical aspects of design, marketing, and content creation, the AI frees up human creators to focus on what they do best—being creative. It democratizes access to advanced creative tools, enabling individuals and small teams to produce work that rivals that of large, well-funded studios. As the 4M AI Model continues to evolve, it is set to become an indispensable tool in the creative professional's arsenal, transforming the way we create, share, and experience content in the digital age.

In the realm of security and surveillance, the 4M AI Model represents a significant leap forward, offering unprecedented levels of precision and efficiency in object detection. Traditionally, security systems have relied on human monitoring and basic motion detection algorithms to identify potential threats or suspicious activities. While these methods have been effective to some extent, they are often prone to errors, such as false alarms, and require significant manpower to manage effectively. The introduction of the 4M AI Model changes this landscape by bringing a level of sophistication and accuracy that was previously unattainable.

The 4M AI Model's ability to integrate and process various types of data—text, images, and spatial information—enables it to detect objects and activities with a high degree of precision. For instance, in a security system monitoring a large facility, the AI can analyze video feeds in real-time, identifying and categorizing objects such as vehicles, people, or packages. But it doesn't stop there; the AI can also recognize specific actions or behaviors that may indicate a security threat, such as a person loitering near a restricted area or an unattended bag left in a public space. By accurately distinguishing between benign and potentially dangerous situations, the 4M AI Model reduces the likelihood of false alarms, allowing security personnel to focus their attention on genuine threats.

Moreover, the 4M AI Model's ability to learn and adapt over time makes it particularly valuable in dynamic environments where threats can evolve rapidly. As the AI is exposed to more data, it becomes better at recognizing patterns and anomalies, improving its accuracy and responsiveness. This adaptability is crucial in settings like airports, train stations, and other high-security areas, where the nature of potential threats can change from day to day. By providing security teams with actionable insights and alerts, the 4M AI Model enhances overall situational awareness, enabling a more proactive approach to threat detection and prevention.

In healthcare, the 4M AI Model is poised to revolutionize the way medical imaging and diagnostics are conducted, offering new possibilities for improving accuracy and treatment planning. Medical imaging has long been a cornerstone of modern healthcare, allowing doctors to diagnose and monitor a wide range of conditions. However, interpreting these images—whether they are X-rays, MRIs, or CT scans—requires a high level of expertise, and even then, there is always a risk of human error. The 4M AI Model addresses this challenge by providing an advanced tool for analyzing medical images with remarkable precision.

One of the key use cases for the 4M AI Model in healthcare is in the early detection of diseases. For example, in the case of cancer, early detection is often critical to successful treatment outcomes. The 4M AI Model can be trained to recognize the subtle signs of malignancies in medical images, identifying tumors at an earlier stage than might be possible with the human eye alone. By doing so, it not only improves the chances of catching the disease early but also reduces the likelihood of false positives, which can lead to unnecessary stress and invasive procedures for patients.

Beyond detection, the 4M AI Model also plays a vital role in treatment planning. Once a condition has been diagnosed, the AI can assist doctors in determining the best course of action by analyzing a patient's medical history, current condition, and even genetic data. For example, in the treatment of complex diseases like cancer, where the effectiveness of different therapies can vary significantly from patient to patient, the AI can help identify the most promising treatment options, personalized to the individual's unique profile. This level of personalized care, guided by the insights provided by the 4M AI Model, represents a significant advancement in precision medicine, where treatments are tailored to achieve the best possible outcomes.

The integration of the 4M AI Model into healthcare systems also has the potential to streamline operations and reduce costs. By automating the analysis of medical images and supporting diagnostic processes, the AI can alleviate some of the workload on healthcare professionals, allowing them to focus on patient care rather than administrative tasks. Additionally, the improved accuracy and efficiency provided by the AI can lead to faster diagnosis and treatment, reducing the time patients spend in the healthcare system and potentially lowering the overall cost of care.

In both security and healthcare, the 4M AI Model stands out as a powerful tool that enhances human capabilities, making critical systems more efficient, accurate, and reliable. Whether it's safeguarding public spaces or improving patient outcomes, the impact of this technology is profound, offering new ways to address some of the most pressing challenges in these fields. As the 4M AI Model continues to evolve, its role in enhancing security and healthcare will likely expand, paving the way for even more innovative applications and improvements in the future.

Chapter 4: Enhancing Everyday Technology

The integration of the 4M AI Model into Apple's voice assistant, Siri, represents a transformative leap in how users interact with technology. Since its introduction, Siri has been a pioneering force in voice-activated AI, capable of handling simple tasks like setting reminders, sending messages, and answering basic queries. However, as user expectations have grown, so too has the demand for a more intelligent and context-aware assistant—one that can understand and respond to complex, multi-faceted requests with ease. The 4M AI Model is poised to meet this demand, elevating Siri's capabilities to a whole new level.

One of the most significant enhancements that 4M brings to Siri is its ability to process and integrate multiple data types—text, images, audio, and even 3D spatial information—into a unified understanding of user commands. This multimodal capability allows Siri to move beyond simply responding to voice commands; it can now interpret and act upon requests that involve different forms of input simultaneously. For example, imagine a scenario where you ask Siri to "Show me the photos from my last trip, remind me of the name of the restaurant we visited, and suggest similar places nearby." The 4M AI Model enables Siri to process this complex query by displaying relevant photos, recalling the contextual information about the restaurant, and providing personalized recommendations—all in one seamless interaction.

The ability to handle such intricate requests is a direct result of 4M's advanced natural language processing (NLP) capabilities, which allow Siri to understand the nuances of human speech more accurately than ever before. Whether it's deciphering multi-part queries, recognizing colloquial language, or understanding context, the 4M AI Model equips Siri with a deeper level of comprehension. This means that Siri can not only execute commands more effectively but also engage in more natural, human-like conversations with users, making interactions feel less robotic and more intuitive.

Beyond improving its understanding of spoken language, the 4M AI Model also enhances Siri's ability to generate meaningful and contextually appropriate responses. For instance, if you ask Siri to "Plan a weekend getaway," the AI can now analyze your preferences, past choices, and current trends to offer personalized suggestions that go beyond the generic. It might recommend destinations, suggest activities based on the season, and even curate an itinerary—all tailored to your unique tastes and needs. This level of personalization, driven by the 4M AI Model's ability to synthesize various data points, makes Siri not just a reactive assistant but a proactive companion that anticipates your needs and desires.

The integration of 4M also empowers Siri to perform tasks that require a combination of verbal and visual input. For example, if you're designing a new living room layout, you could ask Siri to "Place a modern-style couch in the center of the room and add a coffee table in front of it." Using the 4M AI Model's ability to manipulate 3D scenes, Siri could instantly generate a virtual layout based on your description, allowing you to see and adjust the design in real-time. This fusion of natural language commands with visual and spatial reasoning transforms Siri into a versatile tool for creative and practical tasks, far beyond its original scope.

Another area where the 4M AI Model enhances Siri is in its contextual awareness and memory. With 4M, Siri can now remember the context of previous interactions and use that information to inform future responses. For example, if you previously asked Siri for recommendations on a new book to read, and later inquire about the best time to visit a particular city, Siri could suggest a book that matches the theme of your travel plans. This continuity in conversation, supported by the 4M AI

Model, allows Siri to provide a more cohesive and connected user experience, where each interaction builds on the last.

Furthermore, the 4M AI Model's integration into Siri paves the way for more sophisticated use cases, such as accessibility features for users with disabilities. By combining visual, auditory, and textual information, Siri can offer comprehensive assistance to users who may need alternative ways to interact with their devices. For instance, a visually impaired user could receive detailed verbal descriptions of their surroundings captured through their device's camera, while also being able to input commands via voice or text. This multimodal approach ensures that Siri can adapt to various user needs, making technology more inclusive and accessible for everyone.

The transformation of Siri through the 4M AI Model is not just about making Siri smarter; it's about fundamentally changing the way we interact with our devices. By enhancing Siri's ability to understand, respond, and anticipate, the 4M AI Model makes Apple's voice assistant more responsive, intelligent, and human-like. Whether it's managing everyday tasks, assisting with creative projects, or providing personalized recommendations, Siri—powered by 4M—is set to become an even more integral part of our digital lives, offering a seamless and enriched user experience that feels more like a conversation with a trusted companion than a mere interaction with technology.

The integration of the 4M AI Model into ARKit marks a significant advancement in augmented reality (AR) and spatial computing, transforming how users interact with digital content in the physical world. ARKit, Apple's framework for building augmented reality experiences, has already enabled developers to create immersive and engaging applications that overlay digital elements onto the real world. However, the introduction of the 4M AI Model into this ecosystem elevates AR to an entirely new level of interactivity and accessibility.

One of the key challenges in creating compelling AR experiences has been the complexity involved in designing and manipulating 3D environments. Traditionally, developers needed to rely on specialized software and extensive coding to place, move, and interact with virtual objects within a real-world context. The 4M AI Model simplifies this process by allowing users to interact with AR environments using natural language instructions. For example, instead of manually adjusting the position of a virtual object in a room, a user could simply say, "Place a modern chair near the window," and the AI would accurately position the chair based on the user's description.

This natural language integration makes AR more intuitive and accessible, not just for developers but also for everyday users who may not have technical expertise. Imagine a scenario where you're redecorating your living room and want to see how different pieces of furniture would look in the space. With the 4M AI Model, you could verbally describe the arrangement you have in mind, and the AR environment would adjust accordingly, allowing you to visualize the changes in real-time. This ability to interact with AR using everyday language removes the barriers that have traditionally made AR a more niche technology, opening it up to a broader audience.

Furthermore, the 4M AI Model enhances the realism and interactivity of AR experiences by improving the way digital objects interact with the physical world. By processing spatial information more accurately, the AI can ensure that virtual objects behave as they would in reality, considering factors like lighting, shadows, and perspective. This creates a more immersive experience, where the lines between the virtual and physical worlds blur, making AR applications more compelling and believable.

In addition to augmented reality, the 4M AI Model is set to revolutionize creative software like Final Cut Pro by simplifying video editing and production through the use of natural language instructions. Video editing has traditionally been a labor-intensive process, requiring meticulous attention to detail, extensive knowledge of software tools, and significant time investment. The 4M AI Model streamlines this process by allowing users to perform complex editing tasks simply by describing what they want to achieve.

For instance, a video editor could instruct the AI to "Create a highlight reel of the best moments from this footage, add upbeat background music, and apply a cinematic color grade." The 4M AI Model would then analyze the footage, identify the key moments, and automatically compile and edit them into a polished final product. This capability not only speeds up the editing process but also democratizes video production, making it accessible to individuals and small teams who may not have the resources or expertise to produce high-quality videos manually.

The ability of the 4M AI Model to understand and execute natural language commands is a game-changer for creative professionals. It allows them to focus more on their artistic vision and less on the technical intricacies of the editing process. For example, a filmmaker working on a documentary could use the AI to quickly sort through hours of footage, identify the most relevant clips, and assemble a rough cut based on a verbal description of the narrative structure. This level of automation and intelligence reduces the time spent on routine tasks, freeing up more time for creative exploration and refinement.

Moreover, the 4M AI Model's integration into creative software like Final Cut Pro enhances collaboration among teams. With the ability to quickly generate and share drafts or previews based on simple instructions, creative teams can iterate on ideas more efficiently, leading to faster decision-making and a more dynamic workflow. This is particularly valuable in fast-paced industries like advertising or media production, where the ability to respond quickly to client feedback or market trends can make a significant difference.

The impact of the 4M AI Model on both augmented reality and video editing illustrates its potential to transform creative industries by making advanced technologies more accessible and user-friendly. By integrating natural language processing with spatial computing and multimedia editing, Apple is enabling a new era of creativity where users can bring their ideas to life with unprecedented ease and precision. Whether it's designing a virtual space or editing a complex video project, the 4M AI Model empowers users to achieve their creative goals with greater efficiency and flexibility, setting the stage for a future where technology and creativity are more closely intertwined than ever before.

Chapter 5: Accessibility and Inclusivity

The 4M AI Model's multimodal capabilities represent a significant advancement in making technology more inclusive, particularly for users with disabilities. Accessibility has long been a crucial aspect of technological development, and with the integration of 4M AI, Apple is taking a major step forward in ensuring that digital tools and experiences are accessible to everyone, regardless of their physical or cognitive abilities.

One of the key ways the 4M AI Model enhances accessibility is through its ability to process and integrate multiple types of data—text, images, audio, and spatial information—into a single, cohesive system. This allows the AI to adapt to different user needs and preferences, providing a more personalized and inclusive experience. For instance, a user with visual impairments might rely heavily on audio and haptic feedback, while someone with hearing loss might depend on visual cues and text-based information. The 4M AI Model can seamlessly accommodate these varying needs by tailoring its responses and outputs to suit each individual user.

For users with visual impairments, the 4M AI Model offers enhanced capabilities that make interacting with technology more intuitive and informative. By combining computer vision with natural language processing, the AI can provide detailed verbal descriptions of the user's surroundings, captured through the device's camera. For example, a user might ask, "What's in front of me?" and the AI could describe the scene in detail, including the objects present, their positions, and any relevant context. This not only helps users navigate their environment but also enables them to interact with digital content in a more meaningful way, such as identifying objects in photos or videos and understanding visual content on websites or social media.

Additionally, the 4M AI Model can assist users with visual impairments in accessing written information more effectively. By converting text from images or documents into spoken words, the AI allows users to "read" text that would otherwise be inaccessible. This can be particularly useful for reading signs, labels, or printed materials in everyday situations, as well as for consuming digital content such as articles, books, or online posts. The AI's ability to process and understand complex language ensures that these verbal descriptions are not just literal translations but contextually rich and meaningful, enhancing the overall experience.

For users with hearing impairments, the 4M AI Model can improve accessibility by providing real-time captioning and transcription services. By integrating audio and text data, the AI can convert spoken words into written text with high accuracy, allowing users to follow conversations, presentations, or videos even if they cannot hear the audio. This feature is particularly valuable in educational or professional settings, where clear communication is essential. The AI can also be used to translate sign language into text or spoken words, further bridging the communication gap and enabling more inclusive interactions.

The 4M AI Model's multimodal capabilities also extend to individuals with mobility impairments, who may find traditional input methods like keyboards or touchscreens challenging to use. By allowing users to control their devices using natural language commands, the AI reduces the need for physical interaction, making technology more accessible to those with limited mobility. For example, a user could simply speak commands to browse the web, compose emails, or control smart home devices, without needing to physically interact with their device. This not only makes technology more accessible but also empowers users to be more independent in their daily lives.

Moreover, the 4M AI Model's ability to integrate spatial information enhances accessibility for users who may struggle with spatial awareness or navigation. For instance, individuals with cognitive disabilities might benefit from the AI's capability to provide step-by-step guidance through complex tasks or environments. By combining verbal instructions with visual cues, the AI can help users navigate unfamiliar spaces, complete tasks that require spatial understanding, or interact with virtual environments in a way that is tailored to their needs.

The 4M AI Model's focus on inclusivity goes beyond simply making existing technologies more accessible; it also opens up new possibilities for creating tools and experiences specifically designed for users with disabilities. Developers can leverage the AI's multimodal capabilities to build applications that cater to specific accessibility needs, whether it's a navigation app for visually impaired users or an educational tool for individuals with learning disabilities. The flexibility and adaptability of the 4M AI Model make it a powerful platform for innovation in accessibility, enabling the creation of solutions that are more personalized, effective, and user-friendly.

In essence, the 4M AI Model is not just about advancing technology; it's about making sure that these advancements are available to everyone, regardless of their abilities. By integrating multiple forms of data into a single system that can adapt to individual needs, Apple is ensuring that its technologies are more inclusive, empowering users with disabilities to interact with the digital world in ways that were previously difficult or impossible. This commitment to accessibility reflects a broader vision of technology as a tool for empowerment, one that enables all users to connect, create, and engage with the world around them on their terms.

The 4M AI Model introduces a range of inclusive features that are specifically designed to accommodate the diverse needs and preferences of users, particularly those with disabilities. These features leverage the model's multimodal capabilities to create a more accessible and personalized technology experience, ensuring that everyone can benefit from the advancements in artificial intelligence. Here are two key examples of how the 4M AI Model enhances inclusivity:

1. Verbal Descriptions for Visually Impaired Users

One of the most impactful features of the 4M AI Model is its ability to provide detailed verbal descriptions of visual content, making it more accessible to users with visual impairments. By integrating computer vision and natural language processing, the AI can analyze images, videos, and real-world scenes captured through a device's camera, and then generate spoken descriptions that convey the essential details.

For instance, if a visually impaired user is navigating a busy street, they can use their smartphone's camera to capture the surroundings and ask the AI to describe what's in front of them. The 4M AI Model could provide a detailed verbal description, such as, "You are approaching a crosswalk with a pedestrian signal on the right. There's a red car parked on the left side of the street, and a person walking a dog is crossing in front of you." This kind of real-time, context-aware feedback helps users navigate their environment safely and confidently.

Similarly, when browsing the web or using social media, the AI can describe images that appear on the screen, allowing visually impaired users to understand and engage with visual content that would otherwise be inaccessible. For example, when scrolling through a social media feed, a user might encounter a photo posted by a friend. The AI could describe the image, saying, "This is a photo of a sunset over a beach, with orange and pink hues in the sky and waves gently lapping at the shore." This allows the user to share in the visual experience, fostering a greater sense of connection and inclusion.

Moreover, the 4M AI Model's ability to interpret and describe complex scenes extends to areas like shopping and document reading. A visually impaired user shopping online could ask the AI to describe a product image in detail, helping them make more informed purchasing decisions. In a similar vein, the AI can read aloud text from printed documents or signs, enabling users to access information in physical spaces where braille or other accessible formats might not be available.

2. Adaptation to Various User Needs and Preferences

Another standout feature of the 4M AI Model is its ability to adapt to a wide range of user needs and preferences, making technology more customizable and accessible. This adaptability is crucial for ensuring that users with different disabilities or preferences can interact with their devices in ways that best suit them.

For users with hearing impairments, the 4M AI Model can provide real-time transcription of spoken words into text, making conversations, videos, and audio content accessible. For instance, during a meeting or lecture, the AI could transcribe spoken dialogue into text that appears on the user's screen, allowing them to follow along even if they cannot hear the audio. This feature is particularly valuable in educational and professional settings, where clear communication is essential.

Additionally, the AI can generate text-based descriptions of audio content, such as podcasts or voice messages, enabling users who are deaf or hard of hearing to access the same information as those who can hear. The AI's ability to seamlessly convert audio into text helps bridge the communication gap, ensuring that all users can participate fully in conversations and content consumption.

For users with mobility impairments, the 4M AI Model's natural language processing capabilities allow for hands-free interaction with devices. Users can control their smartphone, tablet, or computer by speaking commands, reducing the need for physical input through touchscreens, keyboards, or mice. For example, a user with limited hand mobility could say, "Open my email and read the latest message," and the AI would execute the task without requiring any physical interaction. This hands-free control extends to smart home devices as well, allowing users to manage their environment—adjusting lights, controlling the thermostat, or locking doors—through simple voice commands.

The AI's adaptability also means it can tailor its responses and functionality based on individual preferences. For example, users who prefer a more concise interaction can set the AI to provide brief, to-the-point responses, while those who benefit from more detailed explanations can opt for more in-depth feedback. This level of customization ensures that the technology is not one-size-fits-all but instead meets the unique needs of each user.

In essence, the 4M AI Model's inclusive features are designed to make technology more accessible, personalized, and responsive to the diverse needs of users. By providing verbal descriptions, real-time transcriptions, and hands-free control, the AI empowers individuals with disabilities to interact with their devices and the world around them more independently and confidently. These advancements underscore Apple's commitment to inclusivity, ensuring that the benefits of cutting-edge technology are available to everyone, regardless of their abilities.

Chapter 6: Data Privacy and Security

The 4M AI Model's approach to on-device processing represents a significant shift in how artificial intelligence handles data, with profound implications for user privacy and security. Traditionally, many AI models, especially those requiring significant computational power, rely heavily on cloud processing. This means that data, including potentially sensitive personal information, is sent from the user's device to remote servers for processing and then returned to the device. While cloud processing offers immense computational capabilities, it also introduces vulnerabilities, such as potential data breaches and unauthorized access.

By contrast, the 4M AI Model is designed to perform much of its processing directly on the user's device, significantly reducing the need to transmit data to the cloud. This on-device processing is made possible by the advancements in Apple's custom silicon, particularly the Neural

Engine embedded in its chips, which provides the necessary computational power to run complex AI models locally. This architecture not only enhances the efficiency and responsiveness of AI-powered applications but also provides a substantial boost to user privacy.

One of the key benefits of on-device processing is that it keeps sensitive data closer to the user, minimizing the risk of exposure to third parties. For instance, when a user interacts with the 4M AI Model, whether through voice commands, image analysis, or spatial computing, the data generated during these interactions is processed and stored locally on the device. This approach drastically reduces the amount of personal information that needs to be sent to the cloud, thereby limiting the potential for data interception or unauthorized access during transmission.

Additionally, on-device processing ensures that users retain greater control over their personal data. Since the data does not need to leave the device for processing, users can be more confident that their interactions with the AI remain private and secure. This is particularly important in scenarios involving sensitive information, such as health data or private conversations, where maintaining confidentiality is paramount. The ability of the 4M AI Model to function effectively without relying on external servers underscores Apple's commitment to protecting user privacy while still delivering cutting-edge AI capabilities.

Apple's approach to artificial intelligence is deeply rooted in its broader commitment to user privacy and security. The company has consistently prioritized these values, often positioning itself as a leader in the tech industry's push towards more ethical handling of personal data. Apple's philosophy is that privacy is a fundamental human right, and this principle is reflected in its design and implementation of AI technologies, including the 4M AI Model.

One of the central tenets of Apple's approach to AI is the concept of data minimization. This principle dictates that the company collects only the data necessary to provide a service and ensures that this data is handled in a way that maximizes user control. With the 4M AI Model, this means that Apple is committed to processing as much data as possible on the device itself, without relying on large-scale data aggregation in the cloud. This approach not only enhances privacy but also aligns with Apple's goal of reducing its reliance on user data to deliver personalized and effective AI experiences.

Furthermore, Apple employs robust encryption methods to protect data that must be stored or transmitted. For instance, any data that does leave the device for processing—such as when syncing across devices or accessing cloud-based services—is encrypted both in transit and at rest. This ensures that even if the data were intercepted, it would be nearly impossible for unauthorized parties to decipher it. Apple's end-to-end encryption, particularly in services like iMessage and FaceTime, exemplifies this commitment to maintaining the highest standards of data security.

Apple also emphasizes transparency and user consent in its AI implementations. The company ensures that users are informed about how their data is used and provides clear, accessible options for managing privacy settings. This transparency extends to features like App Tracking Transparency, which gives users the power to control which apps can track their activity across other companies' apps and websites. By putting these decisions in the hands of users, Apple reinforces its commitment to respecting user autonomy and privacy.

The development and deployment of the 4M AI Model within this privacy-centric framework demonstrate Apple's dedication to creating AI that is both powerful and responsible. By prioritizing on-device processing and minimizing data exposure, Apple not only enhances the security of its users' information but also sets a new standard for privacy in the AI industry. This approach is particularly significant as AI becomes more integrated into our daily lives, ensuring that as technology advances, it does so in a way that respects and protects user rights.

In conclusion, the 4M AI Model's emphasis on on-device processing and Apple's overarching commitment to user privacy represent a forward-thinking approach to AI development. By keeping data local and minimizing cloud dependency, Apple is able to offer advanced AI capabilities without compromising the security and privacy of its users. This commitment to ethical AI design is not just a feature; it is a foundational aspect of Apple's technology, reflecting the company's belief that innovation and privacy can—and should—go hand in hand.

Chapter 7: The Public Launch and Community Impact

Apple's decision to make the 4M AI Model publicly accessible through Hugging Face marks a significant departure from its traditionally secretive approach to research and development. Hugging Face, a prominent open-source AI platform, has become a central hub for AI developers, researchers, and enthusiasts to share models, collaborate on projects, and push the boundaries of what AI can achieve. By choosing to release the 4M AI Model on this platform, Apple is not only demonstrating a new level of openness but also signaling its commitment to fostering a more collaborative and innovative AI ecosystem.

The significance of this move cannot be overstated. For years, Apple has been known for its tight control over its technology and intellectual property, often operating behind closed doors until a product is ready for public release. However, by making the 4M AI Model available on Hugging

Face, Apple is embracing a more open and community-driven approach. This openness allows developers from around the world to experiment with, modify, and build upon the 4M AI Model, potentially leading to breakthroughs that Apple alone might not have achieved.

Releasing the 4M AI Model on Hugging Face serves several strategic purposes. First, it allows Apple to engage directly with the broader AI community, gaining valuable feedback and insights that can inform future iterations of the model. The platform's collaborative nature means that developers can contribute to the model's improvement, fixing bugs, optimizing performance, and even adding new features that Apple's internal teams may not have considered. This kind of crowdsourced innovation is incredibly powerful, as it harnesses the collective expertise of a diverse and global community.

Second, by making the 4M AI Model publicly accessible, Apple is helping to democratize AI technology. Traditionally, access to cutting-edge AI models has been limited to well-funded organizations with significant resources. However, by releasing the 4M AI Model on an open platform like Hugging Face, Apple is ensuring that a wider range of developers—including independent creators, startups, and academic researchers—can access and utilize this advanced technology. This democratization of AI tools aligns with Apple's broader mission to empower people through technology, enabling more individuals and organizations to innovate and create impactful solutions.

The collaboration with Hugging Face also has the potential to accelerate the adoption and integration of the 4M AI Model across various industries. As developers begin to experiment with the model and incorporate it into their projects, the range of applications and use cases for the 4M AI Model will expand. This could lead to the development of new AI-powered products and services that leverage the model's unique capabilities, from creative tools and security systems to healthcare solutions and beyond. By making the model accessible to the developer community, Apple is effectively planting seeds for future innovations that could reshape entire industries.

Engaging the developer community through this openness fosters a culture of innovation and collaboration that is essential for the continued advancement of AI technology. When developers are given access to powerful tools like the 4M AI Model, they are not just users—they become co-creators, contributing to the evolution of the technology and exploring its potential in ways that a single company could not achieve alone. This collaborative spirit is at the heart of the open-source movement, where sharing knowledge and resources leads to faster progress and more diverse innovations.

Moreover, by participating in the open-source community through Hugging Face, Apple can help set standards and best practices for AI development. The 4M AI Model's release provides a benchmark for other developers and companies, showcasing what is possible with advanced multimodal AI. Apple's involvement in the community can also influence the ethical development of AI, promoting transparency, fairness, and accountability in how AI models are created and deployed.

The decision to release the 4M AI Model on Hugging Face is not just about sharing technology; it's about building a community of innovators who can collectively advance the state of AI. As developers engage with the model, they will discover new ways to apply its capabilities, pushing the boundaries of what AI can do and exploring its potential to solve real-world problems. This collaborative approach accelerates the pace of innovation, as ideas are shared, tested, and refined in a dynamic and open environment.

In summary, Apple's collaboration with Hugging Face and the public release of the 4M AI Model represent a significant shift towards openness and community engagement in AI development. By making this advanced AI technology accessible to a global network of developers, Apple is not only democratizing AI but also fostering a culture of collaboration that will drive future innovations. This move highlights the importance of community-driven development in the rapidly evolving field of artificial intelligence and positions Apple as a leader not just in technology but in the collaborative spirit that will shape the future of AI.

Chapter 8: The Market Impact of 4M AI

The announcement of the 4M AI Model has had a remarkable impact on Apple's stock performance, with the company experiencing a significant 24% surge in its stock value in the wake of the news. This increase in market valuation reflects the confidence and optimism that investors have in Apple's latest technological innovation and its potential to reshape various industries. The 4M AI Model is not just another product release; it represents a strategic move that positions Apple as a major player in the rapidly evolving artificial intelligence landscape, attracting both market attention and investor enthusiasm.

The 24% increase in Apple's stock performance can be attributed to several factors. Firstly, the 4M AI Model is seen as a groundbreaking advancement in AI technology, capable of integrating multiple modalities—text, images, audio, and spatial data—into a single, cohesive system. This capability opens up a wide range of applications across industries such as healthcare, security, creative arts, and more, all of which are sectors with significant growth potential. Investors recognize that the 4M AI Model could drive new revenue streams for Apple, particularly as the company continues to diversify its product offerings beyond hardware into software and services.

Secondly, the stock surge reflects the broader market's recognition of Apple's ability to innovate and lead in the tech industry. The development of the 4M AI Model showcases Apple's commitment to staying at the forefront of technological advancement, particularly in a field as competitive and transformative as artificial intelligence. This announcement reassures investors that Apple is not only keeping pace with its competitors but is also capable of setting new industry standards, which in turn drives confidence in the company's long-term growth prospects.

Moreover, Apple's strategic partnerships and collaborations, such as the one with Hugging Face, further boost investor confidence. By making the 4M AI Model publicly accessible and engaging with the global AI community, Apple is positioning itself as a leader in the open-source and collaborative development space, which is increasingly seen as essential for driving innovation in AI. These moves suggest that Apple is not only focusing on developing cutting-edge technology but is also keen on building a robust ecosystem around its AI advancements, which could lead to sustained growth and market leadership.

In comparison to its competitors, Apple's AI strategy stands out for its emphasis on user-centric design, privacy, and integration with existing products. Unlike companies like Nvidia, which focuses heavily on providing the hardware infrastructure for AI with its powerful GPUs, or OpenAI, which has gained prominence for developing cutting-edge models like GPT and ChatGPT, Apple's approach is more holistic, integrating AI into its broader ecosystem of devices and services.

Nvidia's strategy revolves around being the backbone of AI development by supplying the necessary computational power through its GPUs, which are essential for training and deploying AI models. Nvidia has successfully positioned itself as a key player in the AI hardware market, catering to industries ranging from gaming and entertainment to deep learning and autonomous vehicles. However, Nvidia's focus is primarily on enabling AI for other companies and developers, whereas Apple is more concerned with how AI can be integrated into consumer products to enhance user experiences.

OpenAI, on the other hand, is known for pushing the boundaries of AI research, particularly in the area of natural language processing. OpenAI's models, like GPT-3 and GPT-4, are among the most advanced in generating human-like text, and the organization's research has had a significant impact on the development of AI capabilities globally. OpenAI's strategy is centered on creating AI that can perform a wide range of tasks autonomously, with a focus on ethical considerations and the safe deployment of AI technologies.

Apple's AI strategy differentiates itself by focusing on making AI more accessible and integrated into everyday life. The 4M AI Model exemplifies this approach by seamlessly integrating text, images, audio, and 3D data into a single system that can be used across Apple's ecosystem of products. Apple prioritizes user privacy, ensuring that AI processing can be done on-device, which reduces reliance on cloud-based systems and enhances data security. This user-centric approach, combined with Apple's emphasis on seamless integration across its devices, positions Apple as a leader in delivering AI that is not only powerful but also deeply embedded in the consumer experience.

Furthermore, Apple's AI strategy is built on the principle of enhancing the functionality and usability of its products without compromising on privacy. This contrasts with the broader industry trend of leveraging large-scale data collection for AI development. By focusing on on-device processing and minimizing data sharing, Apple offers a more privacy-conscious alternative, which resonates with its customer base and differentiates it from competitors who may prioritize data-driven AI development.

In conclusion, the 24% surge in Apple's stock performance following the 4M AI Model announcement underscores the market's confidence in Apple's ability to innovate and lead in the AI space. While Nvidia and OpenAI focus on enabling and advancing AI technologies, Apple's strategy centers on integrating AI into its ecosystem in a way that enhances the user experience while maintaining a strong commitment to privacy and security. This holistic approach not only sets Apple apart from its competitors but also positions it as a key player in the future of AI, driving both technological advancements and market growth.

Chapter 9: The Future of 4M AI and Beyond

As the 4M AI Model sets a new benchmark in the field of artificial intelligence, its influence is likely to spark a series of future advancements that will further reshape the technological landscape. The 4M model's integration of multiple data types—text, images, audio, and spatial information—into a unified, highly intelligent system is just the beginning. Looking ahead, we can anticipate several key developments that will build on this foundation.

One of the most promising areas for future advancement is the refinement and expansion of multimodal AI capabilities. As the technology matures, we can expect AI models to become even more adept at seamlessly blending diverse types of data, enabling them to perform tasks with a higher degree of contextual understanding and nuance. Imagine an AI system that not only processes visual and auditory inputs but also integrates real-time biometric data, environmental factors, and emotional cues to deliver highly personalized and responsive interactions. Such advancements could revolutionize sectors like healthcare, where AI could provide more accurate and timely diagnoses by analyzing a broader array of patient data, or in education, where AI could adapt in real-time to a student's learning style, emotional state, and progress.

Furthermore, the creative capabilities of AI are likely to expand dramatically, inspired by the 4M model's ability to generate images from text and manipulate 3D environments. Future AI systems could push the boundaries of creativity by becoming co-creators with humans, generating novel forms of art, music, and media that merge human imagination with machine precision. These systems might also introduce entirely new forms of creative expression, where AI-generated content evolves dynamically in response to user input, creating immersive and interactive experiences that blur the lines between creator and audience.

As AI becomes increasingly embedded in our daily lives, personalization and adaptability will play a crucial role in future developments. AI systems will likely become more adept at learning from individual user behaviors, preferences, and contexts, enabling them to anticipate needs and provide proactive assistance. For instance, AI-powered personal assistants could learn to manage complex schedules, suggest activities, or even handle routine tasks autonomously, freeing up users to focus on more meaningful endeavors. This level of personalization could also extend to consumer products, where AI tailors features, interfaces, and experiences to align with the unique preferences of each user.

The integration of the 4M AI Model into Apple's product ecosystem will undoubtedly be transformative, as the company seeks to leverage this advanced technology across its range of devices and services. Siri, Apple's voice assistant, is poised to undergo a significant evolution with the 4M AI Model at its core. Siri could become far more than a voice-activated assistant; it could evolve into a comprehensive AI companion capable of understanding and responding to complex, multi-layered commands that involve text, images, and spatial reasoning. This would allow users to interact with Siri in more natural and intuitive ways, whether they are managing their daily tasks, seeking personalized recommendations, or even engaging in creative projects.

The potential for 4M AI to enhance augmented reality (AR) experiences is particularly exciting. As Apple continues to develop its AR platform, including the anticipated release of AR glasses, the 4M model could play a central role in making these experiences more immersive and interactive. Imagine wearing Apple's AR glasses and being able to manipulate virtual objects in your environment simply by describing what you want to see. This could revolutionize industries like interior design, where users could visualize and modify room layouts in real-time, or in education, where students could explore complex scientific concepts through interactive, AR-enhanced lessons.

Creative software such as Final Cut Pro stands to benefit significantly from the integration of the 4M AI Model. Video editing and production, traditionally time-consuming and technically demanding tasks, could be streamlined through natural language commands. A filmmaker could describe the type of scene they want to create, and the AI would handle the technical aspects—cutting, arranging, applying effects—allowing the creator to focus more on their artistic vision. This democratization of professional-grade tools could empower a broader range of users to produce high-quality content, opening up new avenues for storytelling and media creation.

In addition to enhancing existing products, the 4M AI Model could also pave the way for entirely new product categories. For instance, in the realm of health and wellness, AI-powered devices could offer real-time, personalized health monitoring and advice, analyzing a combination of biometric data, lifestyle information, and environmental factors to provide tailored recommendations. Such products could play a crucial role in preventive healthcare, helping users maintain their well-being by identifying potential issues before they become serious.

As these advancements unfold, the ethical implications of AI will become increasingly important. Apple's approach to AI development, as demonstrated by the 4M model, underscores the need for responsible innovation that prioritizes user privacy, security, and fairness. One of the key ethical considerations is the handling of personal data. Apple's commitment to on-device processing with the 4M AI Model ensures that sensitive data remains under the user's control, reducing the risk of exposure to unauthorized parties. This approach not only protects user privacy but also sets a standard for how AI should be designed with security in mind.

Another critical ethical issue is the potential for AI to reinforce or exacerbate biases present in the data it is trained on. Apple's focus on transparency and fairness includes efforts to identify and mitigate biases within the 4M AI Model, ensuring that the technology serves all users equitably. This involves careful selection of training data, continuous monitoring for biased outcomes, and the development of algorithms that strive to be inclusive and non-discriminatory. By addressing these challenges head-on, Apple is working to ensure that its AI technologies contribute positively to society and do not inadvertently perpetuate existing inequalities.

The increasing autonomy of AI systems also raises questions about accountability. As AI begins to make more decisions that affect individuals and society, it is crucial that these systems operate in a transparent and accountable manner. Apple's approach emphasizes human oversight, particularly in areas where AI-driven decisions can have significant consequences, such as healthcare or security. The 4M AI Model is designed to assist and augment human decision-making rather than replace it, ensuring that there is always a clear line of responsibility and that AI remains a tool for empowerment rather than a source of unchecked authority.

Finally, the potential misuse of AI for surveillance, misinformation, or other harmful purposes is an ongoing concern. Apple's commitment to ethical AI development includes stringent guidelines on how its technologies can be used, ensuring that they are not deployed in ways that could harm individuals or society. By setting clear ethical boundaries and collaborating with regulators, policymakers, and the tech community, Apple aims to promote the responsible use of AI while mitigating the risks associated with its misuse.

In conclusion, the 4M AI Model is not just a technological breakthrough; it is a harbinger of future advancements that will shape the evolution of AI and its integration into everyday life. As Apple continues to innovate, the ethical considerations surrounding AI will remain at the forefront of its strategy, ensuring that these powerful technologies are developed and deployed in ways that are responsible, inclusive, and beneficial to all.

Conclusion

The 4M AI Model stands as a testament to the transformative power of artificial intelligence, marking a new era in which technology becomes more deeply integrated into our lives in ways that were once the stuff of science fiction. Its revolutionary impact is poised to reshape various industries, from healthcare and security to creative arts and everyday consumer technology. By seamlessly integrating multiple data types—text, images, audio, and spatial information—into a unified system, 4M AI brings a level of sophistication and contextual understanding that opens up new possibilities for innovation and efficiency.

In healthcare, the ability of 4M AI to analyze complex medical data with precision could lead to earlier diagnoses, more personalized treatment plans, and ultimately better patient outcomes. In security, its advanced object detection capabilities enhance surveillance systems, making them more reliable and less prone to false alarms. For creatives, the AI's potential to generate and manipulate visual content through natural language commands democratizes access to professional-grade tools, empowering more people to bring their artistic visions to life. Across the board, 4M AI is set to make technology more intuitive, responsive, and accessible, changing how we interact with the digital world on a fundamental level.

As you consider the implications of 4M AI in your own life or industry, it's important to recognize the opportunities and challenges that come with such a powerful technology. Whether you are a professional looking to streamline your workflow, a business leader seeking to stay ahead of the competition, or simply someone curious about the future of technology, the 4M AI Model offers tools that can enhance creativity, improve efficiency, and drive innovation. However, it also invites us to think critically about how we integrate AI into our lives, ensuring that we do so in a way that is thoughtful, ethical, and aligned with our values.

Looking to the future, the broader impact of AI on society will only continue to grow. As AI systems become more autonomous and embedded in everyday life, the need for responsible development and deployment becomes ever more pressing. The choices we make today—how we design, regulate, and use AI—will shape the world of tomorrow. It is imperative that we prioritize privacy, fairness, and transparency in AI development, ensuring that these technologies serve to uplift humanity rather than divide it.

In this new era of artificial intelligence, the 4M AI Model represents both a tremendous opportunity and a profound responsibility. As we stand on the cusp of a future where AI plays an increasingly central role in our lives, it is up to all of us—developers, policymakers, businesses, and consumers alike—to guide this technology in a direction that benefits all of society. By embracing the potential of AI while remaining vigilant about its risks, we can ensure that the advancements we make today will lead to a brighter, more equitable future for everyone.

www.ingramcontent.com/pod-product-compliance
Lightning Source LLC
Chambersburg PA
CBHW071947210526
45479CB00002B/842